Workbook

New International Edition

Grade 4

Tara Lievesley, Deborah Herridge
Series editor: John Stringer

YS LEARNING
PEARSON

Pearson Education Limited is a company incorporated in England and Wales having its registered office at Edinburgh Gate, Harlow, Essex, CM20 2JE.

Registered company number: 872828

First published 2003. This edition published 2012.

www.pearsonglobalschools.com

26 25 24 23
IMP 16 15 14 13

British Library Cataloguing in Publication Data
A catalogue record for this book is available from the British Library

ISBN 978 0 43513 381 8

Edited by Janice Curry
Designed by Ian Foulis
Original illustrations © Pearson Education Limited, 2003, 2009, 2012
Illustrated by Ian Foulis, Steve Evans and Ian Escott/Beehive Illustration Ltd
Cover photo/illustration © Science Photo Library Ltd
Printed and bound by CPI Group (UK) Ltd, Croydon CR0 4YY

Acknowledgements
Every effort has been made to contact copyright holders of material reproduced in this book. Any omissions will be rectified in subsequent printings if notice is given to the publishers.

Picture Credits
The publisher would like to thank the following for their kind permission to reproduce their photographs:

(Key: b-botton; c-centre; l-left; r-right; t-top)
Fotolia.com: 50tr; **John Foxx Images:** 75tr

All other images © Pearson Education

Contents

Name: ______________________ Date: __________

My skeleton

Label the bones on the human skeleton below.
Use the words in the box.

skull pelvis ribs humerus ankle wrist
ulna radius shoulder backbone

____

____

____

____

____

____

____

____

____

____

Name: ________________________ Date: ____________

Measuring forearms

Measure the forearms of some people you know. Measure from elbow to wrist. Use the table to record your data.

Name	Age (years)	Length of forearm (cm)

1 Who has the shortest forearm?

____

2 Who has the longest forearm?

____

3 How does your forearm change with age?

____

4 Deva thinks your forearm grows all through your life. Tell him why he is wrong.

____

____

____

Name: ______________________________ Date: ____________

Who has the biggest bones?

Our challenge – How does your age affect how big your bones are?

What we think – We think that the older the person the bigger their bones. Bones continue to grow until the person dies.

What we did –

- We measured forearms from fingertip to elbow.
- We measured five different people from different classes.

How we made it fair – We measured the same way each time, using the same ruler.

Results –

Name	Anya (age 7)	Deven (age 8)	Nisha (age 9)	Miss Shah	Mr Patel
Length of forearm (cm)	13	15	18	23	25

What we found out – We found out that the person with the biggest bone in their forearm was Mr Patel. We think his forearm will go on growing.

Answer these questions:

1 Class 4 are wrong. What are the correct conclusions?

____

2 At about what age do bones stop growing?

______________________ years

3 Imagine Mr Patel's arms kept growing. Draw what he would look like in ten years' time.

Name: ______________________ Date: __________

How strong?

Make round tower shapes using paper, paper clips and sticky tape. Then make towers of other shapes – square or triangular. Test the strength of your towers by putting books on top of them. Use the table below to record the data from your investigation.

The shape of my tower				
The number of books it supported				

How did you make your investigation fair? ______________________

____

____

____

Which was the strongest shape? ______________________

____

Name: ______________________ Date: __________

How my arm works

These diagrams show the muscles in your arm.

Put the labels in the correct places.

triceps contracted **biceps contracted**
triceps relaxed **biceps relaxed**

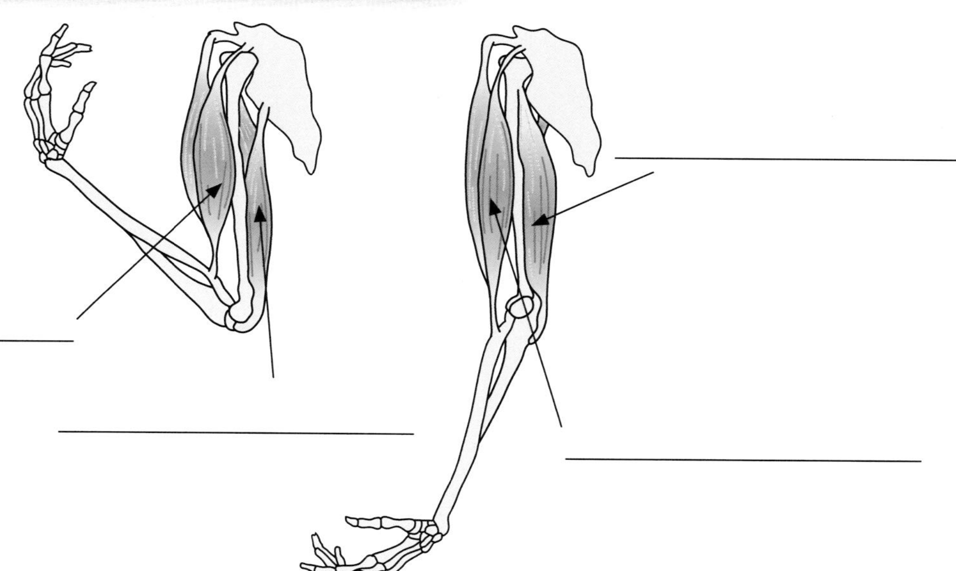

Fill the spaces to explain how your arm moves up and down.

When your ______________ muscle contracts, your ______________ moves up. Your ______________ muscle is relaxed.
When your biceps ______________ relaxes, your arm moves __________.
Your ______________ muscle is contracting.

Name: ______________________ Date: __________

A model arm

You need: 5 soft, bendy wires (such as pipe cleaners or florist's wire), drinking straws and scissors.

1 Feel your hand. How many bones can you count in your fingers?

2 Bend five wires together at one end to make a wire hand.

3 Cut pieces of straw to be the bones. Thread the straws onto the wires.

4 Bend the ends of the wires over.

5 Draw your model hand here.

Name: ______________________ Date: ____________

Drugs as medicine

Look at the pictures. Draw a line from the picture of the medicine to the reason we use it.

Medicine
cough medicine 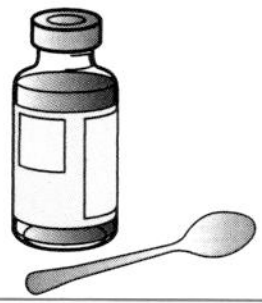
antiseptic cream 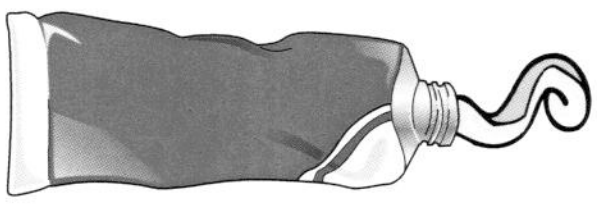
mouthwash 
headache pills 
suncream 
inhaler 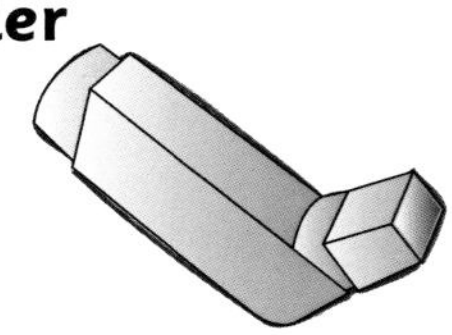

Used for
headache 
bright smile 
cut finger 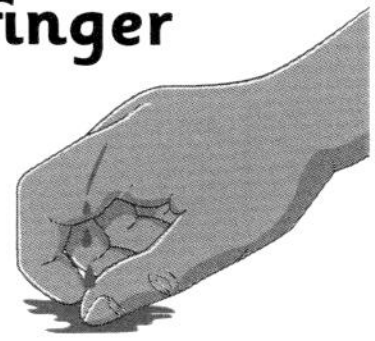
wheezing 
coughing 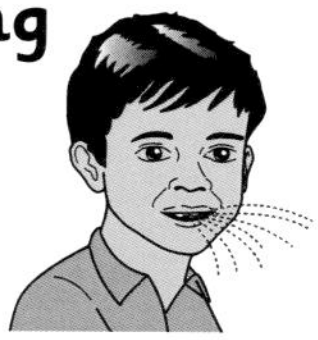
really hot sunny day 

Name: ____________________ Date: __________

Unit 1 assessment

1 Match up these lengths of forearms to the correct person.

5 cm	15 cm	20 cm	12 cm

school student	baby	adult	teenager

2 Label the parts of this skeleton.

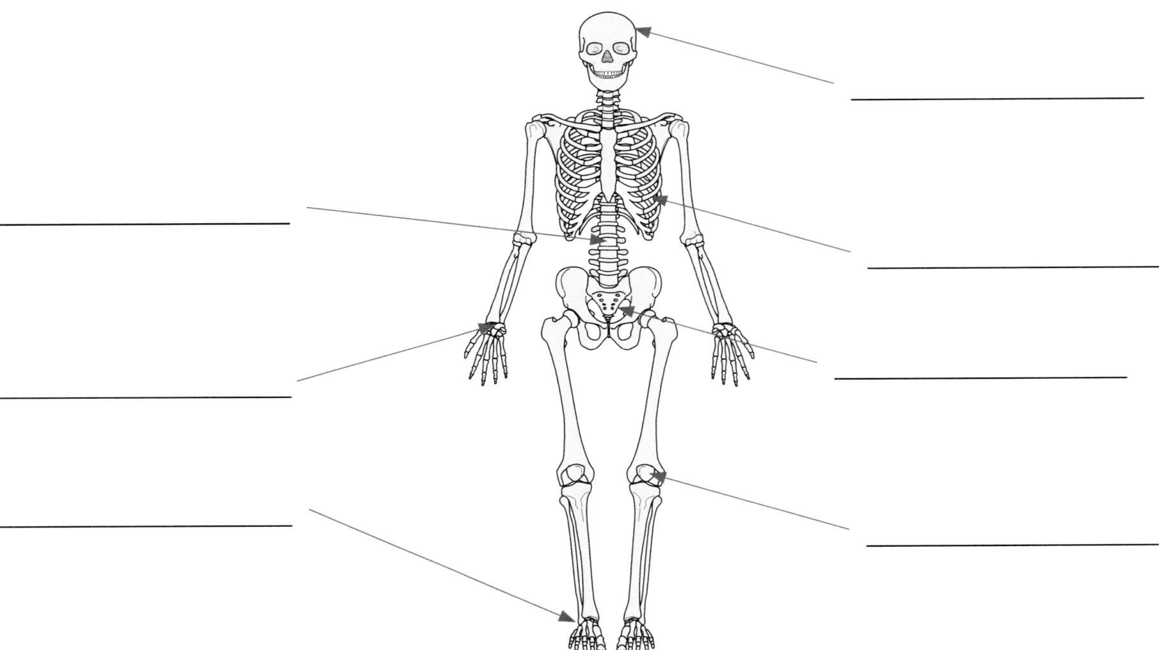

3 Look at this diagram of an arm.

a) Which muscle is contracting, A or B? __________

b) What is the other muscle doing? __________

c) How can you tell? __________

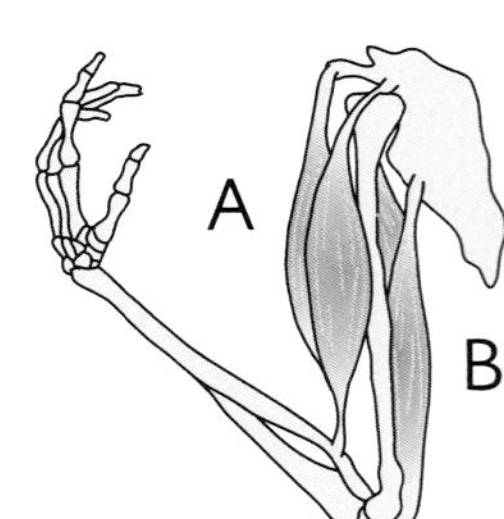

Name: ______________________ Date: ____________

Different habitats

Claude Camel wants to move. He has advertised his habitat:

FOR SALE
Desirable Oasis
Sunny spot.
Warm in the day, cool at night.
Fresh water available.
Dates and leaves to eat.
Thorn bushes when you are really hungry.
Please see Claude Camel for more details.

Pretend another animal wants to sell their habitat.

Write an advertisement for it.

Quick identification

Look at the pictures. Record the information on the table.

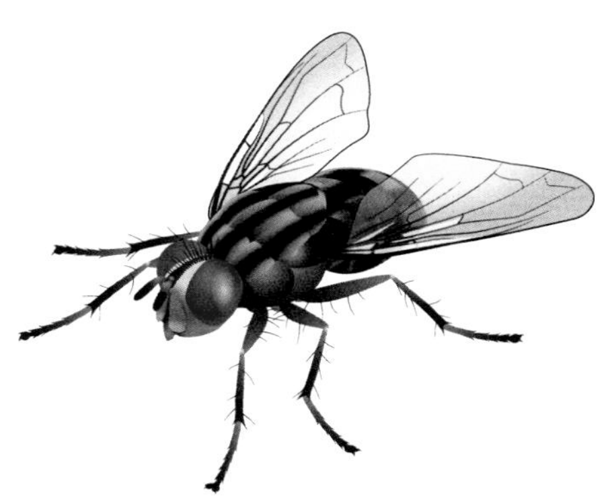

Animal name	Colour of body	Number of legs	Number of wings	Shell	Fur or hair

Plant name	Colour of flower	Number of petals	Thorns or stings	Tall or short	Bark

Name: ______________________ Date: __________

Identifying organisms

1 Choose one animal and one plant.

2 Fill in the spaces below. Put information about your animal or plant.

3 Give your Workbook to a partner.

4 Ask them to draw your animal or plant from the information.

Animal

Shape of body:	
Number of legs:	
Number of wings:	
Shell:	
Skin:	
Colour:	

Plant

Tall or short:	
Leaves:	
Number of petals:	
Colour of flower:	
Thorns or stings:	

How easy was it to draw the organism from the information provided?

____

Name: ______________________ Date: ____________

Grouping living things

Vertebrates are animals with backbones. That is, they have a skeleton inside their bodies. There are five main groups of vertebrates.

1 Join these descriptions to the right group.

Wet skin, fins, lay eggs	birds
Smooth skin, lay eggs, adults can live on land and in water	mammals
Dry skin, lay eggs	amphibians
Feathers, lay eggs	fish
Hair, young born alive, fed on milk	reptiles

2 Camels often walk on soft sand. Why have camels got big, broad feet?

____

3 Camels may get caught in sandstorms. Why have camels got long eyelashes?

____

4 It's a long way between oases. Why have camels got a hump?

____

5 What other animals have these kinds of adaptations?

____

____

____

____

Name: ______________________ Date: __________

Minibeast identification key

1 Use this key to put these four invertebrates in the correct box.

butterfly **ant** **spider** **centipede**

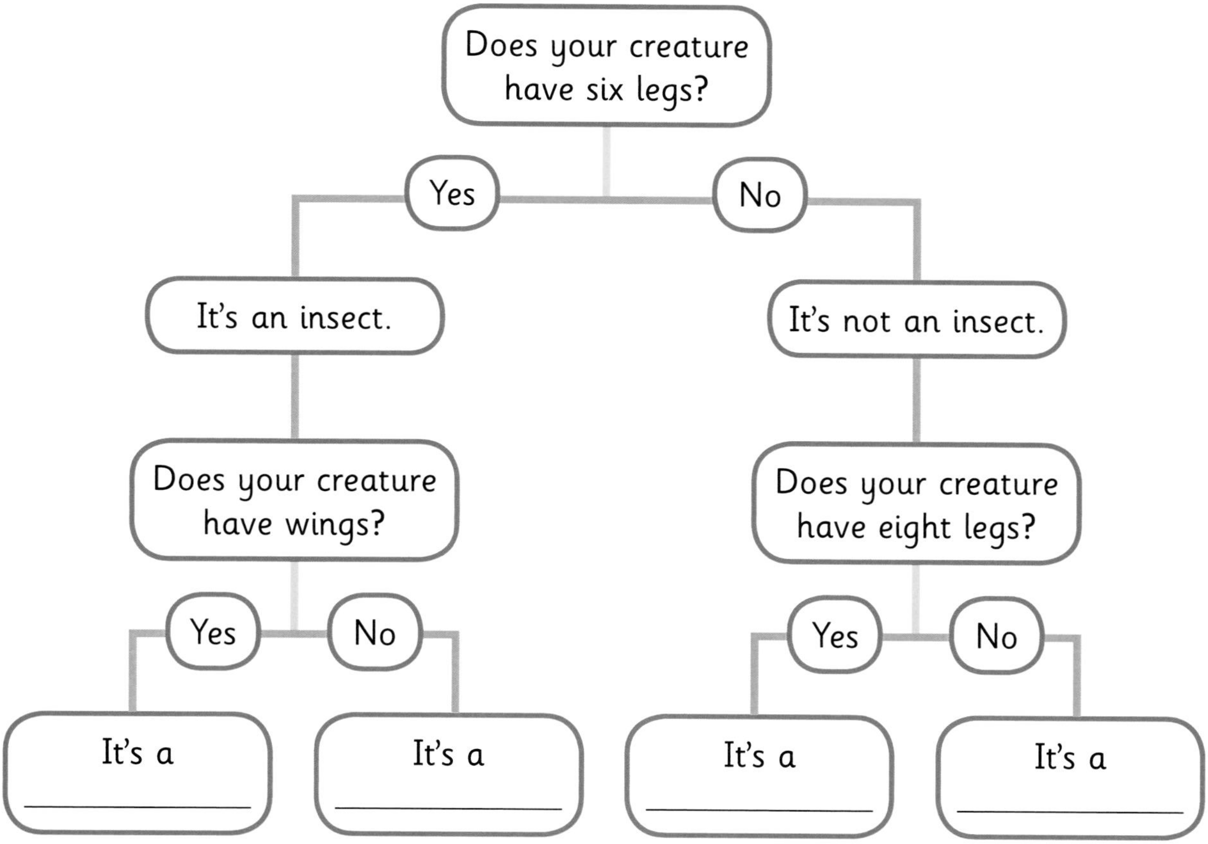

Does your creature have six legs?

- Yes → It's an insect.
  - Does your creature have wings?
    - Yes → It's a ______________
    - No → It's a ______________
- No → It's not an insect.
  - Does your creature have eight legs?
    - Yes → It's a ______________
    - No → It's a ______________

2 Copy the boxes onto paper.
Choose four invertebrates.
Draw and write your own key to identify them.

Name: ______________________ Date: ____________

WS 14

An empty key

Fill in this empty key to identify your own organisms.

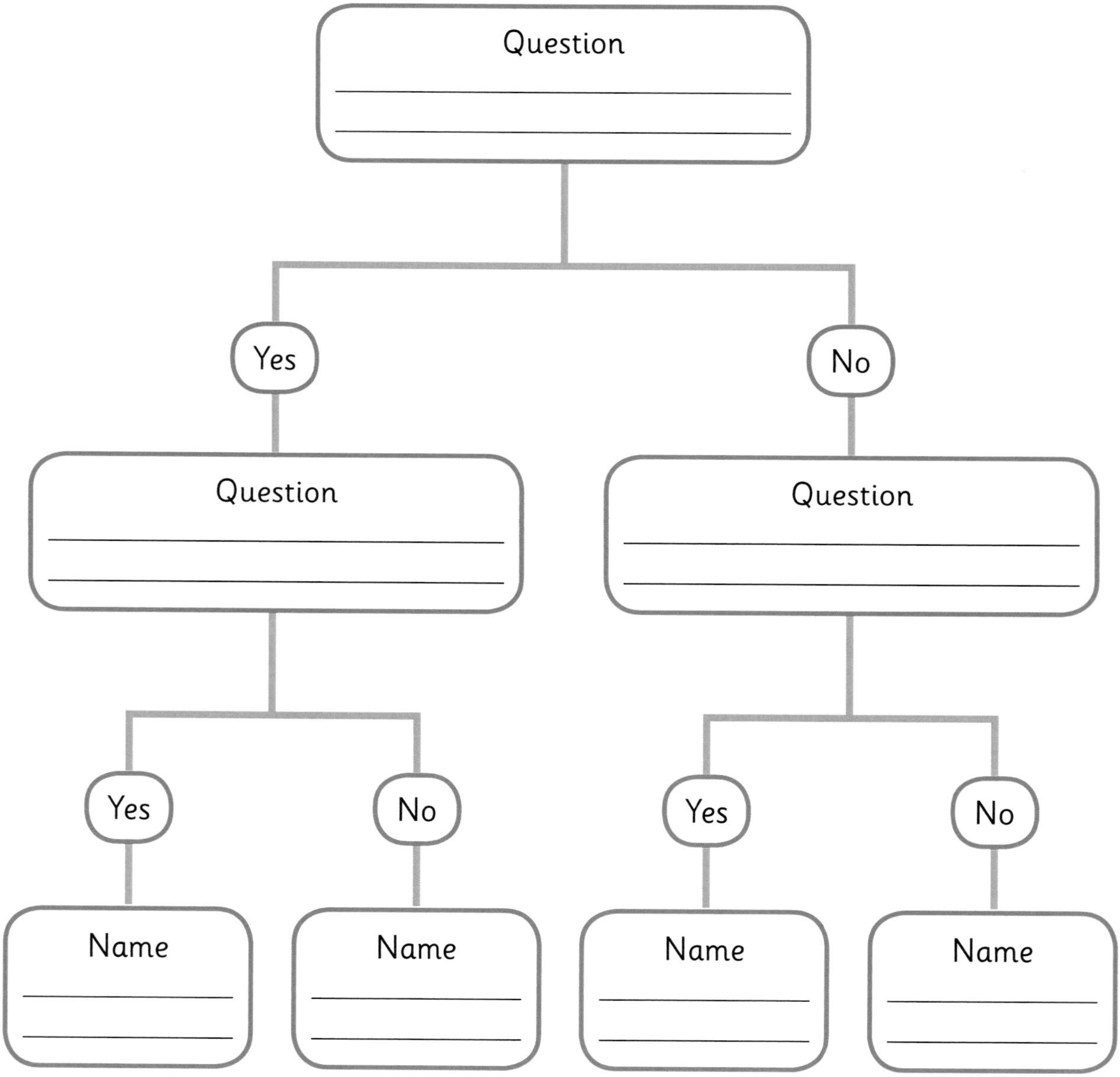
Question
Yes
No
Question
Question
Yes
No
Yes
No
Name
Name
Name
Name

Name: ______________________ Date: __________

Using keys

Ahmed has three friends.

Ahmed

Layla

Farah

Rasheed

1 Think of one of the four friends. Get a friend to ask you questions you can answer with 'yes' or 'no', like these:

- Are you thinking of a girl?
- Are they tall?

Can your friend identify who you are thinking of?

2 Now draw a branching key to identify each of Ahmed's friends.

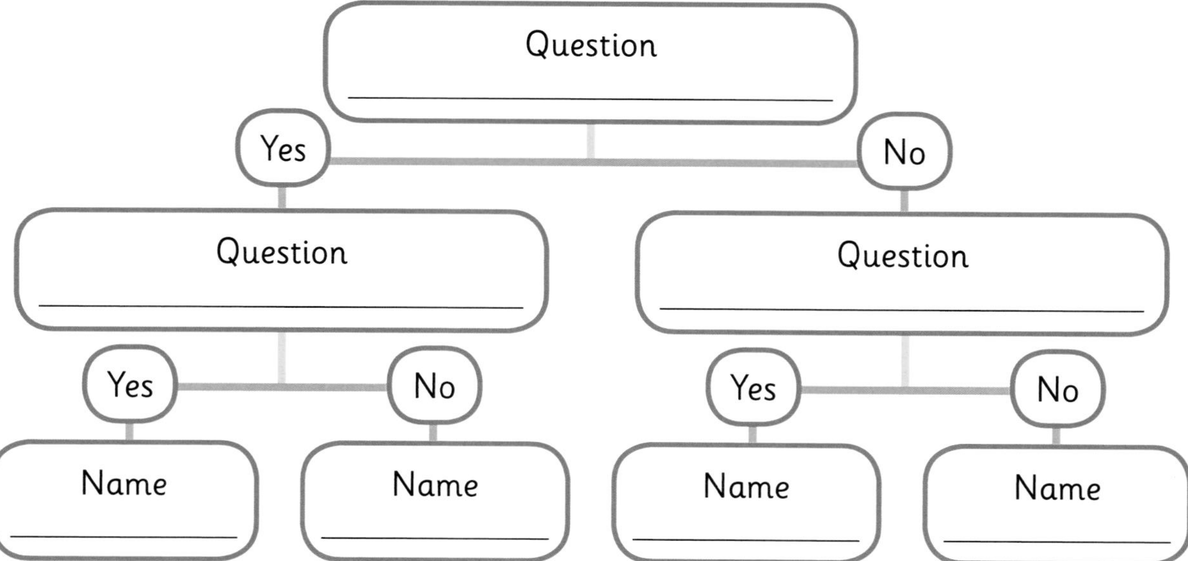

Name: ______________________ Date: __________

Investigating invertebrates

Scientists record their discoveries.
They can look for patterns in their results.
They can see if the evidence supports their predictions.
It helps them remember!

Tables are a good way of recording results.
Tables save writing.

1 Use this table to record where you found your invertebrates.

Where we found our invertebrates	How many we found in that place

2 Use this table to record their choice of food.

Our invertebrates' choice of food	How many chose that food

3 What patterns can you see? Complete these sentences:

a) Our invertebrates chose a habitat that was ______________________.

b) Our invertebrates chose food that was ______________________.

Name: ______________________ Date: __________

Class 4's report

Class 4 reported on their discoveries with invertebrates.

We chose to look for snails. There is a place at the back of the school where you can find them. We found ten snails there. We found three snails in other places.

Mrs Shah asked us why we found ten snails on the wall behind the bushes. We thought it was because it was dark there.

We put our snails in a tank with damp soil and different foods. We gave them biscuit, bread and lettuce leaves. Twelve snails ate lettuce leaves. One did nothing. We think the snails chose lettuce because they like the green colour.

Answer these questions:

1 Give two more reasons why snails might choose a damp, leafy place.

The place was ______________ and ______________ .

2 Give two reasons why snails might choose lettuce leaves to eat.

Lettuce leaves are ______________ and ______________ .

3 What patterns can you see in Class 4's results?

____

4 What three things have you learned about snails?

____

____

____

Name: ______________________ Date: __________

Investigating caterpillars

The students were asked to find out which leaves caterpillars choose to eat. They each had ten caterpillars and three different leaves.

Sanjay gave all ten caterpillars the choice of three different leaves.

Nikhil put food at both ends of his box of ten caterpillars. Then he counted how many went to each end.

Kavya used ten caterpillars and three leaves, like Sanjay. She covered the box with black paper in case they went to the light or the shadow.

Arna used just one caterpillar. 'This is Cliff the amazing caterpillar!' said Arna. 'Offer Cliff different leaves and Cliff will always choose this one!'

1 What is Sanjay doing well?

____

____

2 Why won't Nikhil find the whole answer?

____

____

3 What is especially good about Kavya's idea?

____

____

4 Why isn't Arna's idea very good?

____

____

Name: ____________________ Date: __________

Making food chains

Choose four pictures from the selection below to make a complete food chain. Then, draw each part of the food chain in the diagram at the bottom of the page. Label each picture with the terms 'energy source', 'producer', 'predator' and 'prey'.

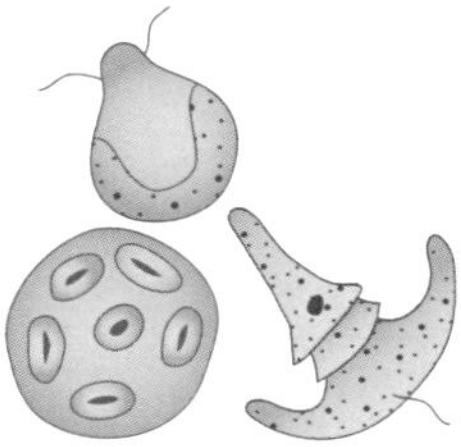

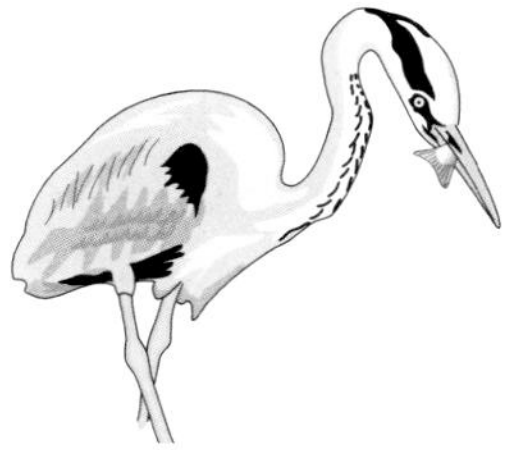

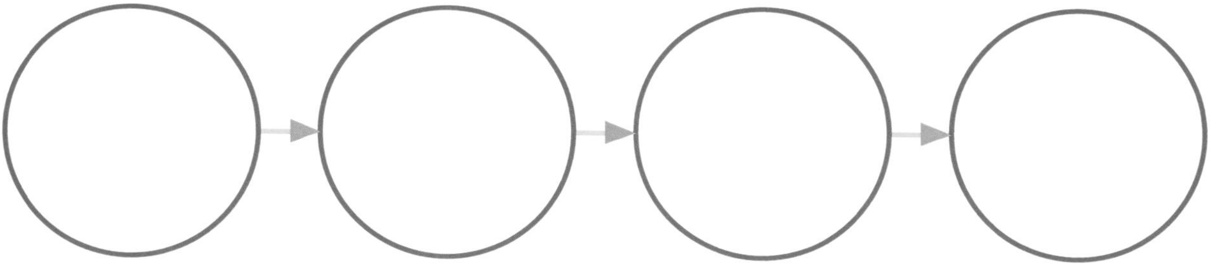

Name: ______________________ Date: ____________

Food chains

The students were playing a chasing game. They each had the name of a food chain stage on their back.

Aminata said: 'I'm the Sun. You can't eat me. But what do I do?'

Bouba said: 'It's good fun being a hawk.'

Edi said: 'It's no fun being a rabbit!'

Jay said: 'Grass doesn't eat anything!'

1 What four names did the students wear?

____

2 Put them in order to make a food chain.

____

3 Which is the producer?

____

4 Which animal is the prey?

____

5 Which is the predator?

____

6 Why does the food chain need the Sun?

____

____

____

7 Draw your own food chain with three or four links in the box.

Name: ______________________ Date: ____________

Our environment

Look at the pictures. Say how these everyday products could either be re-used or recycled.

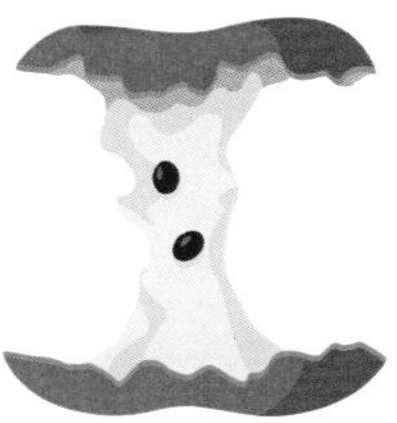

_______________ _______________ _______________

_______________ _______________ _______________

Draw something else that can be recycled.

Name: ______________________ Date: ____________

Unit 2 assessment

1 Where might you find a fish living?

____

2 What part of their body do these animals use to push themselves through water?

a) Duck ______________________________

b) Salmon ______________________________

3 Put some of these into a food chain.

Sun algae water salmon otter (green plants) insect

a) Which is the producer in this food chain? ______________

b) Which are the consumers? ______________

c) Which are the predators? ______________

4 Add three questions to this key so that it correctly identifies the insects.

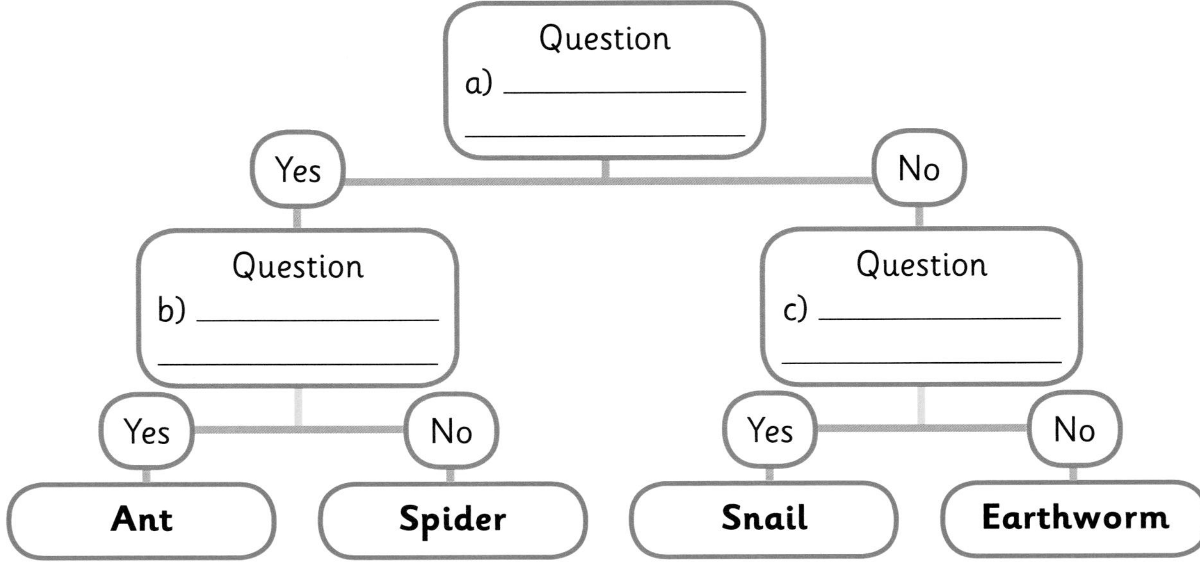

Name: ______________________ Date: ____________

What's the temperature?

1 Look at the thermometers below and write what temperature they are showing.

A
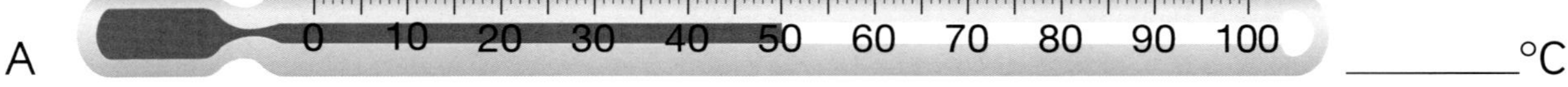

________°C

B
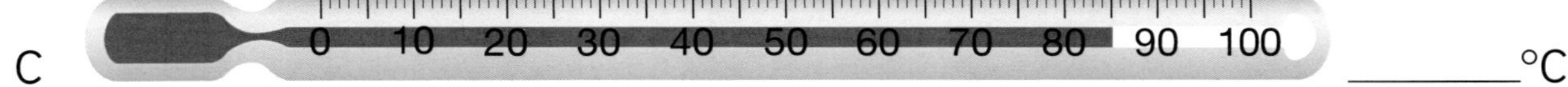

________°C

C
0 10 20 30 40 50 60 70 80 90 100
________°C

Which thermometer shows the hottest temperature? ________

2 Now draw these temperatures on the thermometers below.

0 10 20 30 40 50 60 70 80 90 100
40°C

0 10 20 30 40 50 60 70 80 90 100
55°C

0 10 20 30 40 50 60 70 80 90 100
62°C

Name: ______________________ Date: __________

Classroom temperatures

1 Where do you think is the warmest place in your classroom? Why?

____

2 Where do you think is the coolest place? Why?

____

3 Record your results in the table.

Place	Temperature in °C

4 Draw a bar chart of your results. Label the axes first.

Title: ______________________________

0

Name: ______________________________ Date: ____________

Temperatures at home

1 Look around your home for hot and cold places.

DON'T touch anything very hot or very cold.

DON'T play with electrical switches or devices.

2 Complete these sentences:

a) My oven's highest temperature is ____________ °C.

b) My freezer's lowest temperature is ____________ °C.

c) My air-conditioning is set at ____________ °C.

d) My fridge keeps food at ____________ °C.

e) The warmest place in my home is ________________________ .

f) The coolest place in my home is ________________________ .

Name: ______________________ Date: __________

Lolly insulation

Use this table to write what you think will happen.

How will I wrap my lolly?	Estimated length of lolly (cm)
I won't!	
Cling film	
Foil	
Newspaper	

Use this table to record the results from your investigation.

How I wrapped my lolly	Length of lolly (cm)
I won't!	
Cling film	
Foil	
Newspaper	

Were your predictions correct?

____

____

Name: ______________________ Date: __________

How to keep lollies frozen

Our challenge – To find out if the lolly wrapper affects how long the lolly stays frozen.

What I think – I think that the foil will keep the lolly frozen longest.

What I did –

- I put each lolly in a different wrapper.
- I waited for 20 minutes.
- I measured the lollies afterwards.
- The one that had melted the most will be shortest.

How I made it fair – I used the same type of lolly.

Results –

Method of insulation	Cling film	Foil	Newspaper	None
Length of lolly (cm)	12	13	14	11

1 I found that ______________________________________

____

____

2 How could Farida see if lollies last longer in different places?

____

____

____

Name: ______________________ Date: ____________

Investigating insulators – drawing a bar chart

When your data is in words and numbers, you can only draw a bar chart.

1 If you recorded the temperature changes in different containers, you will have words and numbers. Record your data in the table.

Container	Temperature in °C

2 Now use your data to draw a bar chart.

Title: ______________________

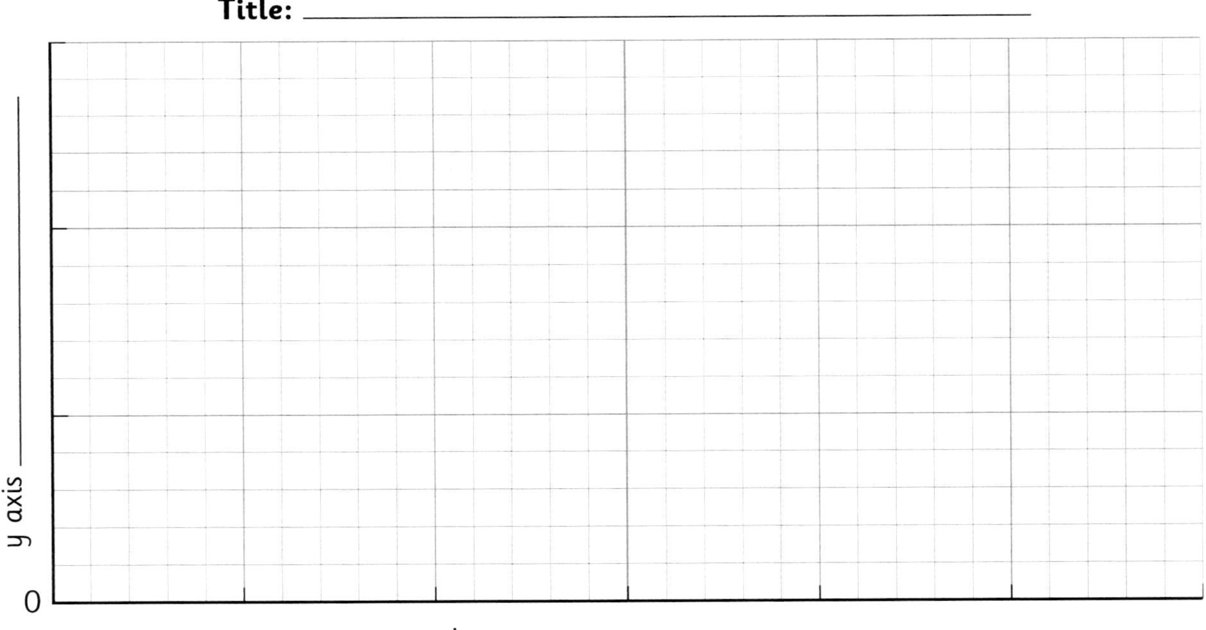

Name: ______________________ Date: __________

Investigating insulators – drawing a line graph

When your data is all in numbers, you can draw a line graph.

1 If you recorded the temperature changes in one container over time, you will have numbers. Record them in the table.

Time in minutes	Temperature in °C

2 Now use your data to draw a line graph.

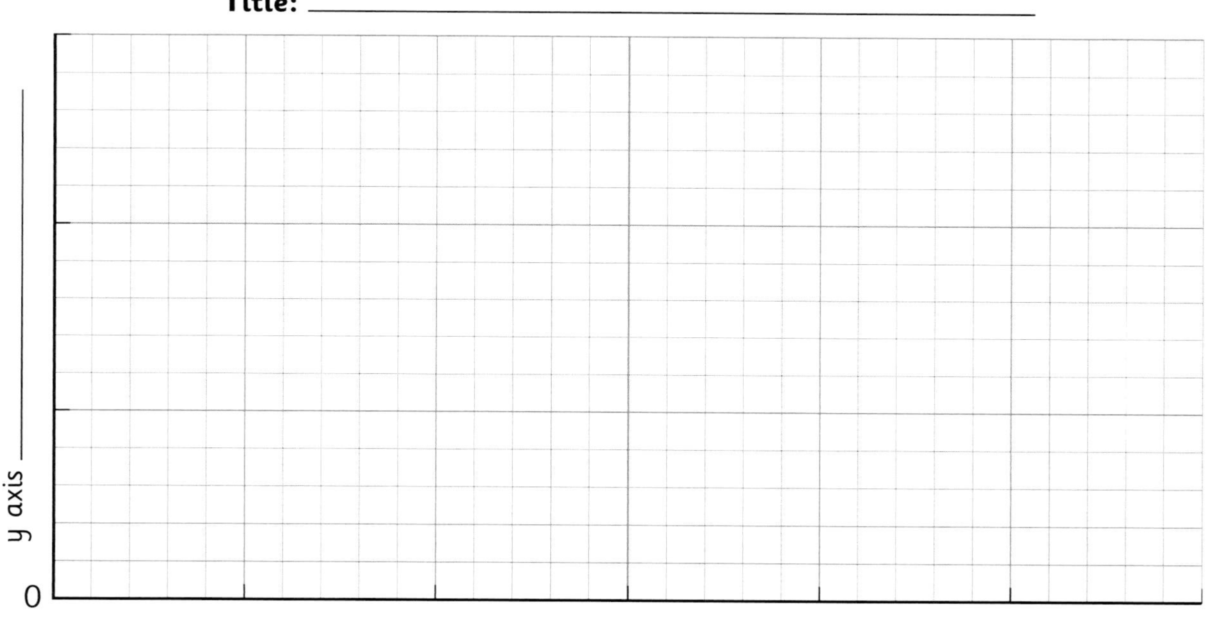

Name: ______________________ Date: ____________

Runny honey

Use this table to record the results from your investigation into which materials are good thermal conductors.

Type of spoon	Time taken for honey to melt (seconds)

Now draw a bar chart of your results.

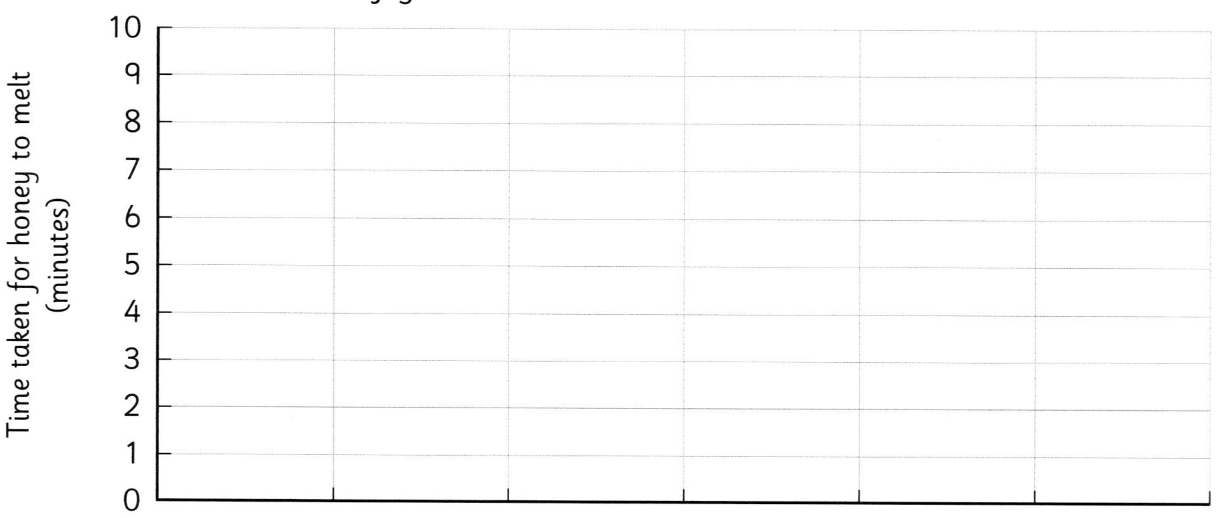

Name: ______________________ Date: __________

Conducting heat

Tariq watched his mother cook. She had three pans on the cooker. One had a metal handle. One had a wooden handle. One had a plastic handle. All three pans were hot.

1 Which pan had the hottest handle?

____

2 Why was this handle hot?

____

3 Which pans had cool handles?

____

4 Why were these handles cool?

____

5 Tariq's mother stirred the food. Why did she use a wooden spoon?

____

Draw and label the pan and spoon you would use to make a hot meal. Label the materials.

Name: ______________________ Date: __________

Unit 3 assessment

1 What is temperature a measure of? ______________________

2 Aditi and Ishaan were making a snack for tea. They each had a cup of tea and a bowl of ice cream. Their mother called them to the table to eat it, but they wanted to finish watching a cartoon.

a) Write down the temperature you think their tea and the ice cream are. Don't forget the units.

Tea ______________ Ice cream ______________

b) Why weren't they very happy when they reached the table 10 minutes later?

____

____

c) What temperature will tea become if it is left for 1 hour?

____

3 Write down the temperatures shown on these thermometers.

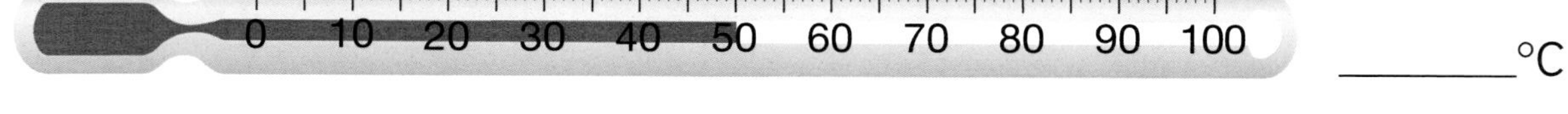

_______°C

_______°C

_______°C

4 What can a thermometer be filled with? ______________________

Name: ______________________ Date: __________

Mystery materials

Use this table to record the results of your investigation into sorting materials into solids and liquids.

Mystery material	Has its own shape (or can be piled up)?	Keeps a level surface when tipped?	Forms drips when poured?	Liquid or solid?
1				
2				
3				
4				
5				
6				
7				
8				
9				
10				

Name: ______________________ Date: __________

Captain's report (1)

Today I had to find a cure for a deadly disease. A spy had removed all the labels on the first aid kit and so I asked the Doctor for help. What did the correct medicine look like? Was it a solid or a liquid? It was too dangerous to taste the materials.

What I did –

- I tested each material in turn using the Doctor's instructions.
- I tried to use the same amount of each material.
- I did the same tests on each material.

Results –

Mystery material	Has its own shape (or can be piled up)?	Forms drips when poured?	Keeps a level surface	Liquid or solid?
1	yes	no	no	solid
2	no	yes	yes	liquid
3	yes	can't pour	no	solid
4	no	yes	yes	liquid
5	yes	can't pour	no	solid
6	yes	no	no	solid
7	no	yes	yes	liquid
8	yes	no	no	solid
9	no	yes	yes	liquid
10	yes	no	no	solid

What I found out – I found that all the liquids had similar properties. I found that all the solids had similar properties, but I still wasn't sure which was the correct medicine. I need to do more tests!

Do you think this is a good report? Explain your reasons.

____

____

Name: ______________________ Date: __________

Solids and liquids

1 Aisha had four materials to test. She called them materials 1, 2, 3 and 4. Help her decide if each was a solid or a liquid.
Tick (✓) the right box.

Material number	Property	Solid?	Liquid?
1	Hard		
2	Can be cut up into different shapes		
3	Pours to give a flat top		
4	Keeps its shape		

2 Complete the table. Show whether each material is a solid or a liquid.

Material	Has it got a shape?	Does it drip when you pour it?	Does it pour to make a level surface?	Is it a solid or a liquid?
Water				
Sand				
Wood				
Honey				

Name: ______________________ Date: __________

Heating materials

Use these tables to record the results from your investigation into what happens when food is heated and then left to cool.

Test material	What happened when it was heated

Test material	What happened when it was left to cool

Name: ______________________ Date: __________

Riya's tests

I tested food. I wanted to see which food melted fastest.

What I did –

- I put pieces of food in cake cases.
- I floated the cake cases on hot water.
- I recorded my results in this table.

Test material	What happened when it was heated
butter	melted quickly
margarine	melted slowly
vegetable fat	melted quickly
milk chocolate	melted quickly
dark chocolate	melted slowly
jelly cube	melted really slowly
ice cube	melted fastest

1 Name three things I had to keep the same.

____

____

____

2 I took the melted food out of the hot water. Which food did not harden again?

____

Name: ______________________ Date: __________

Changing materials

Riya's mum lit a candle.

Here is what she saw:

A candle is white and smooth.

A burning candle gives out heat and light.

There are two parts to the candle flame.

There is bluish unburnt gas in the middle of the flame.

There is a yellow-orange flame around the gas.

There is a puddle of wax in the top of the candle.

There is soot (black powder) at the tip of the flame.

Hot wax runs.

Runny wax hardens at the bottom of the candle.

1 Underline the sentences that describe a solid.

2 Circle the sentences that describe a liquid.

Name: ______________________ Date: __________

Separating materials (1)

1 Are these statements true or false?

a) Pieces of dissolved solids go through a filter. **True / False**

b) Pieces of undissolved solids go through a filter. **True / False**

c) Liquids can go through a sieve. **True / False**

d) Small pieces of solids can go through a sieve. **True / False**

e) Big pieces of solids can't go through a sieve. **True / False**

f) Most liquids can go through a filter. **True / False**

g) A filter is like a sieve with very tiny holes. **True / False**

2 How would you separate:

a) sand and water?

____

____

b) sand and paper clips?

____

____

c) salt and water?

____

____

d) sand and marbles?

____

____

Name: ________________________ Date: __________

Separating materials (2)

The teacher mixed salt and sand. Then she stirred them into water.

She asked her students to do the same. Then she asked them to get the salt, the sand and the water back.

She gave her students:

- salt and sand mixed in warm water from the tap
- a spoon
- a filter funnel
- a thin cloth
- a container

She muddled her instructions.

Write them out in the correct order.

- Collect the water in a container.
- Leave the water on the radiator.
- Stir the salt and sand into the water.
- Pour the water through the filter.
- Line the funnel with the thin cloth.

1 First: ________________________

2 Second: ________________________

3 Next: ________________________

4 Then: ________________________

5 Finally: ________________________

Name: ______________________ Date: __________

Mixing materials with cold water

Use this table. Record the results of your investigation into mixing solids with water.

Sample substance	Appearance after one minute when mixed with cold water

Present your findings in groups.

Name: ____________________ Date: __________

Captain's report (2)

Medicine D51 is a solid that dissolves completely in cold water. I have my six solids. I am going to add each one to cold water, and stir.

1 What must I keep the same?

____

____

2 What shall I observe?

____

____

Results –

Sample substance	Appearance after one minute when mixed with cold water
1	Turns water cloudy, white powder sinks to the bottom of beaker.
2	Some of the solid disappears but most stays in lumps.
3	Solid sinks to the bottom of beaker.
4	Some frothing, most of the solid remains undissolved.
5	Solid disappears completely.
6	Solid dissolves but turns liquid white.

3 Which solid is D51?

____

4 How do I know?

____

Name: ______________________ Date: __________

Dissolving solids

Some materials dissolve in water. Some do not.

1 Put these materials in the correct place in the table:

**sugar   marbles   chalk   brown sugar   sand   Lego bricks
instant coffee   jelly crystals**

Will dissolve in water	Will not dissolve in water

2 You are dissolving lumps of salt in water.

Which of these will help to dissolve the salt faster?

Tick (✓) them.

a) Use colder water.

b) Use warmer water.

c) Stir the water.

d) Stand the water on the table.

e) Break up the lumps of salt.

Name: ______________________ Date: __________

Unit 4 assessment

1 Circle the solid materials.

paper	water	air	sand	sugar cube
milk	ice	plastic ruler	rain	tree

2 Mansoor dropped some materials onto a hot frying pan. He wrote down what he saw in this table.

Name the materials that show solids changing to liquids.

Material	What I saw
chocolate drop	spreads out
plain biscuit	did not move, no change
butter	spreads out, starts to bubble
cooking oil	spreads out

____

3 What do we call the process when a solid changes to a liquid?

____

4 What would Mansoor need to do to turn the liquids solid again?

____

5 What equipment would you use to separate a mixture of flour and raisins?

____

6 Explain what happens when a substance dissolves in water.

____

____

7 Circle the equipment you would use to separate a mixture of sand and water.

sieve	filter paper	colander

Name: ______________________ Date: __________

Air around us

1 Fareed's little sister doesn't believe that air is real.

'You can't see it. You can't smell it. You can't taste it. And it doesn't do anything.'

'Oh, yes it does!' said Fareed. 'Let's go and fly your kite.'

How would you show Fareed's sister that air exists? Complete these sentences.

Without air, yachts would ______________________ .

Hurricanes and tornadoes ______________________ .

Flags flap because ______________________ .

Smoke doesn't go straight up because ______________________ .

2 Draw a picture of a windy day. Show that the wind is blowing in three ways.

Name: ______________________ Date: __________

Air spaces

1 Put three different soils into three containers. Fill them up to the 50 ml mark.

2 Pour water into each container from a measuring jug until the cylinders are full to 100 ml mark.

3 Record how much water each takes.

Material	Water need to fill cylinder in ml
Sand	
Clay	
Compost	

4 Which container takes the most water?

____

5 Which container has the largest air spaces?

____

Name: ______________________ Date: __________

Which soil is best for a wormery?

Earthworms need air. Do different soils hold different amounts of air?

What we did –

- We measured 50 ml of each soil into a measuring cylinder.
- We added water from a measuring jug. We filled each cylinder to the 100 ml mark.

Results –

Soil type	Volume of water needed to fill cylinder (ml)	
	First try	**Second try**
Sand	85	80
Clay	60	62
Compost	90	88

1 Which soil has the most air spaces?

____

2 Why is this a good soil for earthworms?

____

3 Earthworms eat soil. Why is the soil with most air spaces not a good soil for them?

____

Name: ______________________ Date: __________

Professor Vapour's notes

The Professor has been investigating the gases **chlorine**, **oxygen**, **hydrogen** and **carbon dioxide**. His notes have got muddled up. Which gas is each piece of information about?

made by plants and found in air

____

lightest gas, once used in balloons

____

used by plants for photosynthesis

____

needed for things to burn

____

we breathe small amounts of it out

____

can be used as a swimming pool disinfectant

____

makes up a fifth of the air

____

smells and is green-yellow

____

makes lemonade fizzy

____

puts out fires

____

Name: ______________________ Date: __________

Gas information cards

Record Professor Vapour's information from WS 48 about each gas on the cards below.

Name of gas: ______________
1 ______________
____
2 ______________
____
3 ______________
____
Find one more fact about this gas.
____
____

Name of gas: ______________
1 ______________
____
2 ______________
____
3 ______________
____
Find one more fact about this gas.
____
____

Name of gas: ______________
1 ______________
____
2 ______________
____
3 ______________
____
Find one more fact about this gas.
____
____

Name of gas: ______________
1 ______________
____
2 ______________
____
3 ______________
____
Find one more fact about this gas.
____
____

Name: ______________________ Date: __________

States of matter

The sentences in the table describe solids, liquids and gases.

Put an 'S' next to those that describe solids.

Put an 'L' next to those that describe liquids.

Put a 'G' next to those that describe gases.

Careful! Some describe more than one!

These are kinds of materials.	
These have no shape.	
These take the shape of their container.	
These are difficult or impossible to squash.	
These can be cut and shaped.	
These condense to a liquid.	
These fill any open space.	
These cannot be cut and shaped.	
These melt to a liquid.	
These evaporate to a gas.	
These make a point when poured.	
These make a flat top when poured.	
These are very easily squashed.	
These can be squashed with difficulty.	
These have a definite shape.	

Name: ______________________ Date: __________

Unit 5 assessment

1 For each property write the state of matter it describes – **solid**, **liquid** or **gas**.

a) Keeps its shape and its volume ______________________

b) Flows but keeps its volume ______________________

c) Easily squashed ______________________

d) Evaporates ______________________

2 Hamid and Yasmin drew a line around a puddle. They wanted to see how it changed through the day.

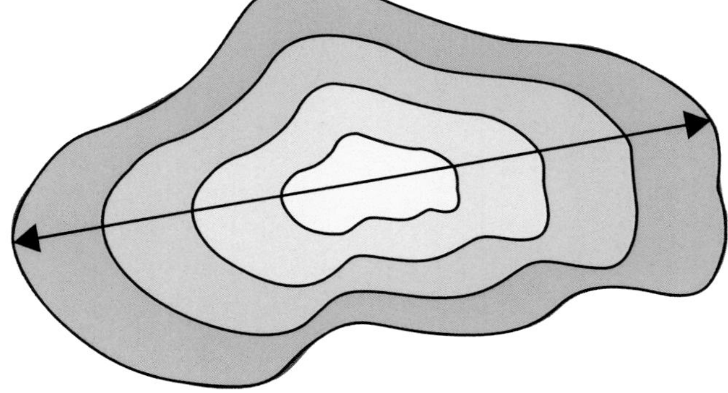

a) What two measurements could they take?

____

____

b) How will the puddle change? ______________________

____

c) Why will it change? ______________________

____

3 Name the gases that are:

a) Essential for burning, respiration and life ______________________

b) Essential for photosynthesis, puts out fires and found in fizzy drinks

____

c) Put in 'lighter-than-air' balloons ______________________

Name: ______________________ Date: ____________

Making a bulb light up

Our challenge – How does a bulb light up?

What we think – We think that all you need to make a bulb light up is a wire and a battery. The wire takes the electricity from the battery to the bulb.

What we did –

- We made drawings of circuits we thought would work.
- We tested our circuits.

Drawings of circuits –

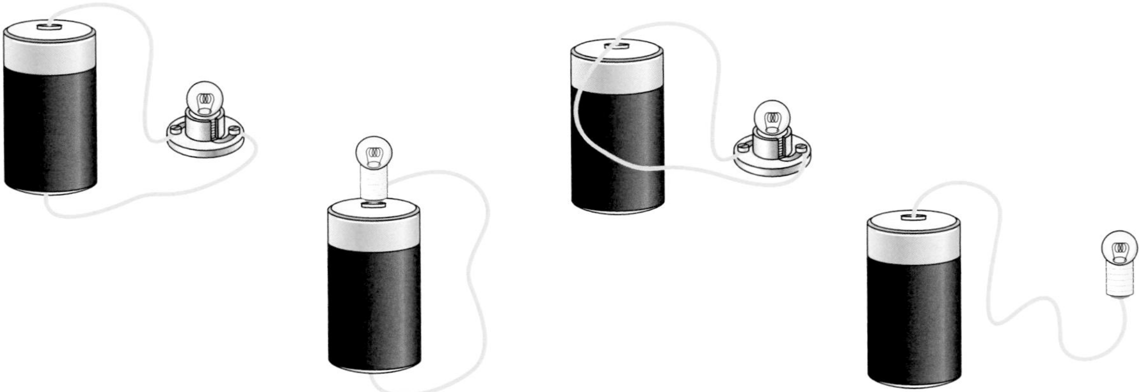

Here is what the students found out. Put the correct words in to complete their work.

We found that not all the bulbs ______________ . The circuits that worked had ______________ wires. One wire connected the ______________ to the bulb. The other wire went ______________ to the battery.

This is called a ______________ circuit. Electricity flows from the ______________ to the ______________ and back to the ______________ .

Name: ______________________ Date: __________

Investigating circuits

Zinah was making changes to a simple circuit.

She connected a battery to a bulb.

She put a switch in the circuit.

Then she made these changes.

Underline what happened.

1 When she closed the switch, the bulb **got dimmer** / **got brighter** / **went off** / **came on**.

2 When she opened the switch, the bulb **got dimmer** / **got brighter** / **went off** / **came on**.

3 When she took the battery out of a circuit, the bulb **got dimmer** / **got brighter** / **went off** / **came on**.

4 When she put two batteries in the circuit, the bulb **got dimmer** / **got brighter** / **went off** / **came on**.

5 When she put another bulb in the circuit, so that there were two, the first bulb **got dimmer** / **got brighter** / **went off** / **came on**.

6 When she unscrewed the new bulb, the first bulb **got dimmer** / **got brighter** / **went off** / **came on**.

Name: ______________________ Date: ____________

Which materials conduct electricity?

Predict which materials you think will conduct electricity by writing them in the hoops.

Conducts electricity	Conducts electricity poorly	Does not conduct electricity

Use this table to record the results of your investigation into which materials conduct electricity.

Material	Conducts electricity? Yes/no

Name: ______________________________ Date: ____________

Materials that conduct electricity

The students predicted which materials would conduct electricity.

Materials	PREDICTION Conducts electricity? Yes/no	RESULTS Conducts electricity? Yes/no
metal paper clip	yes	
birthday card	no	
pencil eraser	no	
plastic toothbrush	no	
steel scissors	yes	
silver necklace	yes	
aluminium foil	no	

1 Complete the table.

2 Make a general rule:
All ______________________ conduct electricity.

3 What do you call materials that do not conduct electricity?

____

4 Name three materials that do not conduct electricity.

____

____

____

Name: ______________________ Date: __________

Conductors and insulators

1 Here are some materials. Some conduct electricity well and some do not. Write the name of each material in the right place in the table.

steel rubber plastic copper wood wool iron aluminium

Electrical conductor	Electrical insulator

2 The wiring in your home is surrounded by plastic.
Tick (✓) two reasons why.
Because it looks good.
Because it protects you from electric shock.
Because it makes the wire easier to bend.
Because it prevents short circuits.

3 Plastic switches can break. Why not make them out of metal?
Tick (✓) two reasons why not.
Because metal is a good insulator.
Because metal is a good conductor.
Because metal is shiny.
Because metal breaks easily.
Because you would get a shock from a metal switch.

Name: ______________________ Date: __________

Making a switch

The students made their own switch.

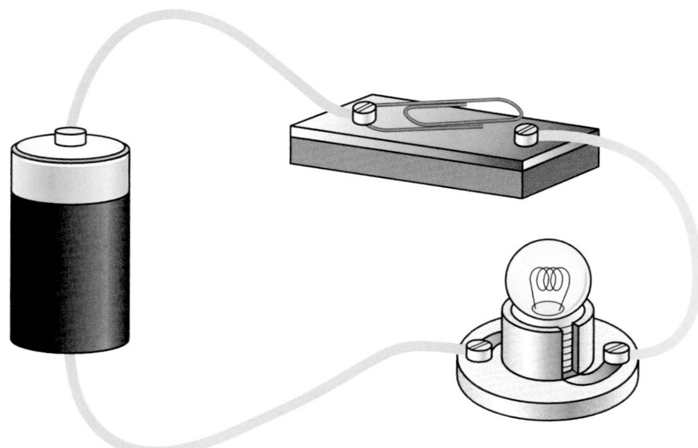

1 What will happen when the paper clip touches the screw?

____

2 Name three parts of the circuit that are conductors.

____

3 Name three parts of the circuit that are insulators.

____

4 Name two objects you could use in place of the paper clip.

____

Name: ______________________ Date: ____________

Morse code

Here is the Morse code. Morse is a system of long or short sounds (or flashes of a bulb). A short sound is shown by a dot and a long sound by a dash.

A	.–	M	––	Y	–.––
B	–...	N	–.	Z	––..
C	–.–.	O	–––	1	.––––
D	–..	P	.––.	2	..–––
E	.	Q	––.–	3	...––
F	..–.	R	.–.	4	....–
G	––.	S	...	5	.....
H	....	T	–	6	–....
I	..	U	..–	7	––...
J	.–––	V	...–	8	–––..
K	–.–	W	.––	9	––––.
L	.–..	X	–..–	0	–––––

Write a simple message both in Morse code and in English.

Morse code: ______________________

English: ______________________

Now write a reply to your message.

Morse code: ______________________

English: ______________________

Name: ______________________________ Date: ____________

Designing switches

Some switches close the gap in a circuit until you open it again.
Some switches close the gap while you hold them closed.

1 Here are some electrical things. Some stay switched on. Some need to be pressed to work. Put them in the right place in the table.

doorbell **television** **reading light** **radio** **electric drill** **television controller** **computer keyboard** **washing machine**

Stays switched on	Switch must be pressed to work

2 How do switches work?
These words are missing. Put them in the right gaps.

electricity **powerful** **insulator** **gap**

Air is a good electrical ______________________ .

Only very ______________________ electricity can travel a short way through air.

A switch puts an air ______________________ in the circuit.

The ______________________ cannot jump the gap.

Name: ______________________ Date: ____________

What affects the brightness of a bulb in a circuit?

Use this table to record the data from your investigation into the effect of adding bulbs to a circuit.

Number of bulbs	Brightness of the bulbs
1	
2	
3	
4	
5	

Now fill in this chart to show your results clearly:

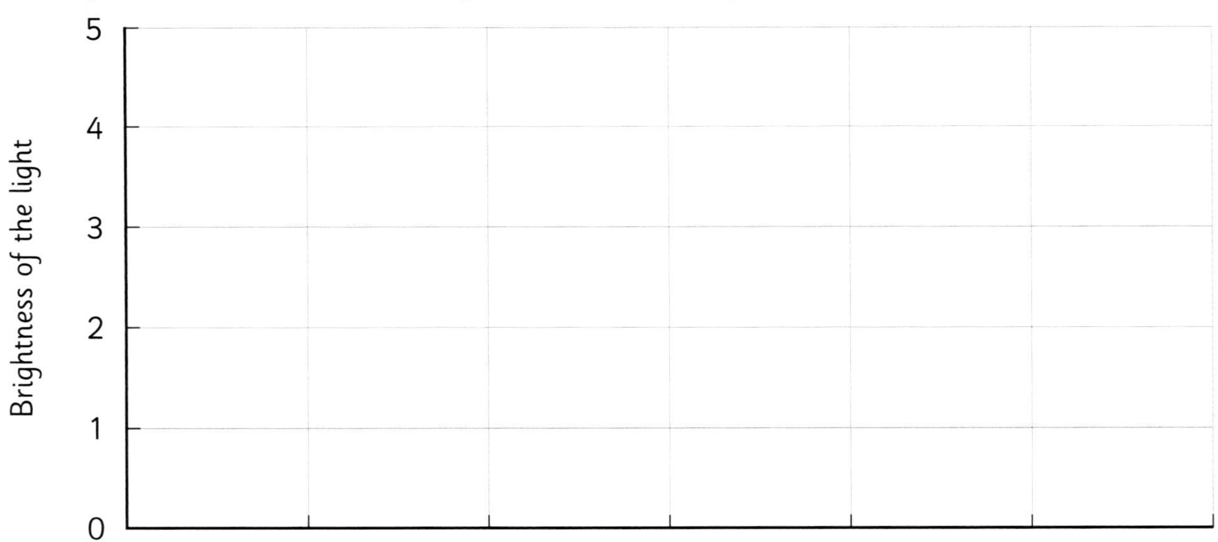

Name: ____________________ Date: __________

Zafar's report

Zafar changed the number of bulbs in a circuit. He found that changed the brightness.

Number of bulbs in the circuit	Brightness of the bulbs
1	extremely bright
2	bright
3	dim
4	very dim
5	can't see any light

1 The more bulbs in a circuit, the ____________________ .

2 The fewer bulbs in a circuit, the ____________________ .

If you put too many batteries in a circuit, you can blow the bulbs. So predict:

3 The more batteries in a circuit, the ____________________ .

4 The fewer batteries in a circuit, the ____________________ .

Name: ______________________ Date: __________

Brighter bulbs

Here are some simple circuits.

All the bulbs are the same.

Circle the correct answer to the question about each circuit.

1 Battery – bulb – back to the battery

Will this bulb light? **Yes** / **No**

2 Battery – bulb – bulb – back to the battery

These bulbs will be **brighter** / **dimmer** than one bulb.

3 Battery – battery – bulb – back to the battery

This bulb will be **brighter** / **dimmer** than a bulb with one battery.

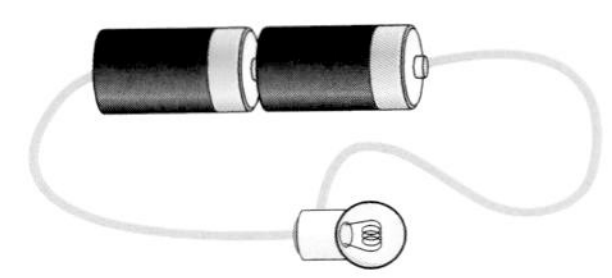

4 Battery – bulb – bulb – bulb – back to battery

The first bulb will be **brighter than** / **dimmer than** / **the same as** the other bulbs.

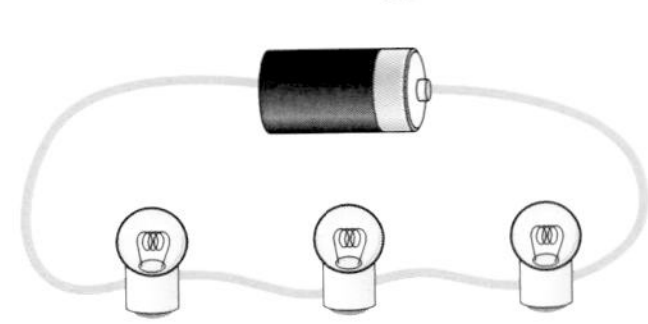

5 Battery – bulb – bulb

The first bulb will be **brighter** / **dimmer** / **off**.

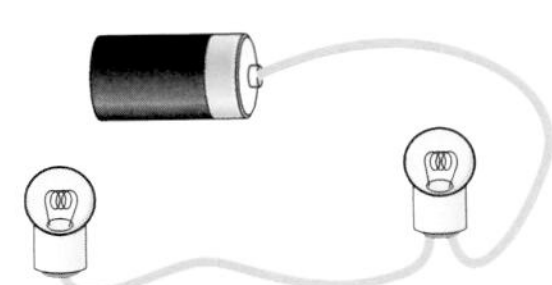

6 Neema drew a circuit with a switch in it.

Which bulbs will light when each switch is closed?

Tick (✓) them.

a) Battery – switch – bulb – bulb – back to the battery

b) Battery – bulb – switch – bulb – back to the battery

c) Battery – bulb – bulb – switch – back to the battery

Name: ______________________ Date: ____________

Mapping magnetism

You need:

A bar magnet and a magnetic compass, a sheet of paper and a pencil.

1 Put the bar magnet in the middle of the paper. Slide the compass close to it. Watch how the compass needle moves.

2 Draw round the compass and lift it away. Now draw the way the needle was facing on the circle.

3 Put the compass on the paper and draw the needle again – and again. Notice how the needles are facing. These directions are the magnets' lines of force. Together, these lines make up the force field.

Now make a record of the lines of force.

1 Put a magnet under a piece of paper. Ask your teacher to sprinkle some iron filings on the paper.

2 Tap the paper gently. Watch as the filings line up to show the force field.

3 Put a wet paper towel on the filings.

4 Wait a day until it has dried out. Blow off the filings and you will have a picture of the force field in rust.

DO NOT handle iron filings. You might rub them in your eyes.

Name: ______________________ Date: __________

Unit 6 assessment

1 Put a tick (✓) next to the materials that will let electricity through.

Material	Lets electricity through
paper	
copper coin	
felt square	
aluminium foil	
wood	

2 What do we call a material that:

a) lets electricity flow through it?

____

b) does not let electricity through?

____

3 Explain why the outside of a plug is made of plastic but the pins are made of metal.

____

____

____

4 Here are two circuits containing switches. In which circuit will the light be lit? Why?

____

____

____

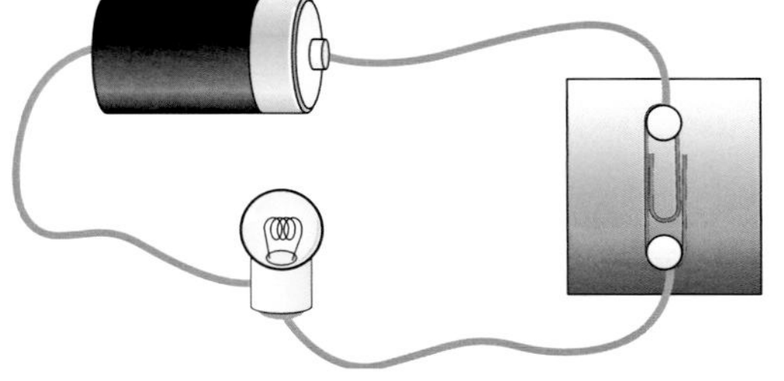

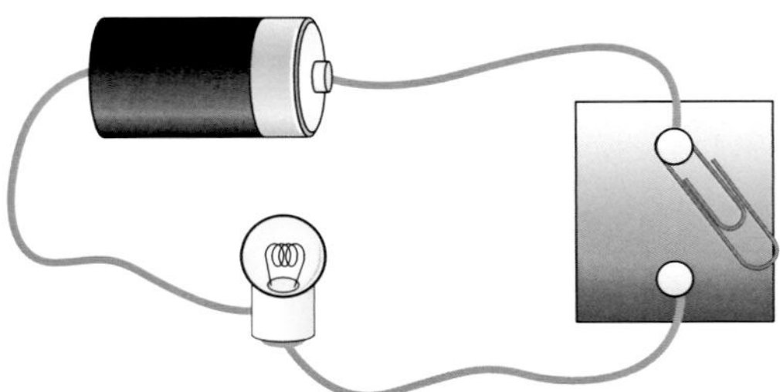

Name: ______________________ Date: __________

Speed of sound

Which travels faster – sound or light?

Ask a friend to go to the far end of the playground, then drop a flag and blow a whistle at the same time.

Record what you observe.

First, I heard/saw ______________________.

Then, I heard/saw ______________________.

Use your observations to explain these:

1 You see a hammer hit before you hear the bang, because

______________________.

2 You see lightning before you hear thunder, because

______________________.

See if you can find answers to these questions:

3 The speed of light is ______________________ km/second.

4 The speed of sound through air is ______________________ km/second.

5 Find out the speed of sound through a solid and a liquid.

____

Name: ______________________ Date: __________

Making sounds

The students compared the sound through air, wood and water.

1 a) Sound travels best through ______________________ .
b) Sound travels worst through ______________________ .

2 Their teacher gave them three speeds of sound – through air, water and metal. They were all in metres per second – m/sec.
She asked the students to put them in the right places in the table.
Sound travels at 1400 m/sec
Sound travels at 330 m/sec
Sound travels at 5000 m/sec

Material	Sound travels through this material at:
Air	
Water	
Metal	

3 Light can travel through outer space. But sound cannot. Explain why.

Sound cannot travel through outer space because ______________________

____

____

____

Name: ______________________ Date: __________

Identifying materials that sound travels through

Use this table to record the data from your investigation into how well sound travels through materials.

Material	Volume of sound

1 Complete these sentences.

a) We found that sound travels better through ______________________ than through ______________________ .

b) The particles in ______________________ are closer together than in ______________________ .

2 Explain why that makes it easier for sound to travel.

____

____

____

Name: ______________________ Date: __________

Listening through materials

1 Are these statements true or false?

a) Sound travels better though air than through water. **True / False**

b) Sound travels better through solids than through liquids. **True / False**

c) Sound travels faster through solids than through gases. **True / False**

d) The speed of sound is different in different materials. **True / False**

2 Explain why you cannot hear well underwater at the swimming pool.

____

____

____

____

Name: ______________________ Date: __________

String telephones

You need: 2 clean plastic pots (e.g. yoghurt pots) with a small hole in the bottom of each, long pieces of different types of string, paper clips.

Thread the string through the bottom of both of the pots and knot paper clips on the inside. The paper clips stop the string pulling through the holes.

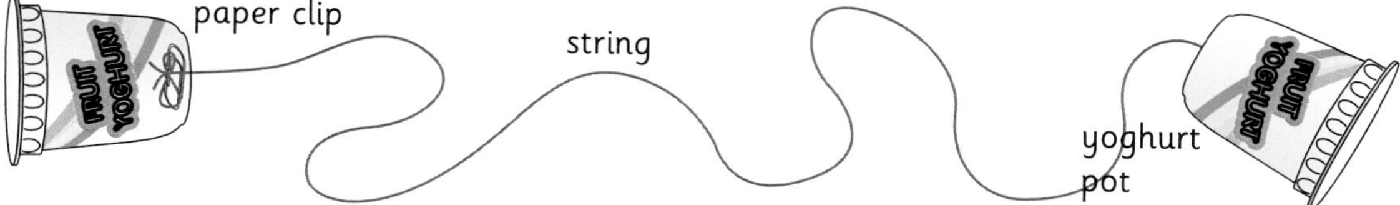

With a friend, pull the string tight. Take it in turns to talk into one pot while your friend listens in the second pot. Don't forget:

- Keep the string stretched tight.
- Keep your fingers off the string.
- Speak softly, but clearly.

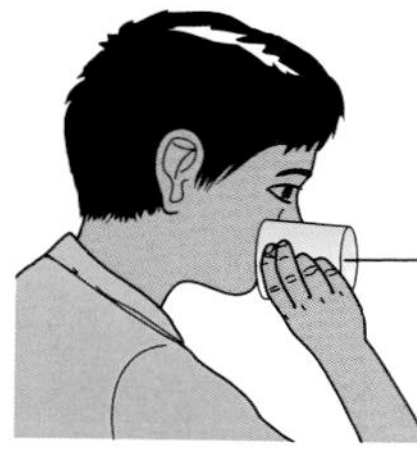

Find out which type of string is the best. Test how clearly you can hear your friend talking. Make a table of your results.

Which string is best? ______________________

Why do you think this is? ______________________

Try using different pots but keep the string the same. Which type of pot is best?

____

Name: ______________________ Date: ____________

Which materials muffle sound the most?

Put something noisy in a box. Wrap it in different materials. Which muffles sound best?

Test material	Sound heard

Which material muffles sound the best? Why do you think that is?

____

____

____

____

Name: ______________________ Date: __________

Making a soundproof box

I have a box, an alarm clock and some different materials. I want to find out which is the best material to muffle sound.

1 What should I do?

____

____

2 What should I change?

____

3 What should I observe or measure?

____

4 What must I keep the same?

____

____

Test material	Sound heard
no soundproofing	
sheet of bubble wrap	
carpet	
foam	
cotton wool	

5 What did I find out?

____

____

Name: ______________________ Date: __________

Noise pollution

What is the noisiest place in your school? Here is a way to find out. Set a portable radio playing softly – no headphones! Take it to different places in the school. Ask a partner to walk away from you until they can't hear the radio any more. Measure how far they are standing away from you. Record the results.

Place	Distance (m)
Playground at playtime	
Playground during lessons	
Staff room	
Classroom	
Dining hall at lunchtime	
Head's office	
Corridor	
Library	

Which of these statements is correct?

a) The greater the distance, the noisier the place. **True / False**

b) The greater the distance, the quieter the place. **True / False**

Explain your answers.

____

____

Name: ______________________ Date: __________

Muffling sound

The makers of Noisy Toys want to send their toys through the post. They have to muffle the sound the toys make.

They have three possible muffling materials:

- **Newspaper**
- **Cotton wool**
- **Bubble wrap**

How can they find which is best at muffling sound?
Tick (✓) the one right answer to each question.

1 What should they change?

a) The toy they test.
b) The material they use.
c) The size of the material they use.
d) The box they pack the toy in.

2 What should they measure?

a) How big the box is.
b) The size of the material they use.
c) The sound they hear when the toy is wrapped.
d) The sound the toy makes before it is wrapped.

3 What must they keep the same?

a) The material they use.
b) The toy they test.

4 Noisy Toys found the following results:

Wrapping material	Sound when the toy is wrapped
Newspaper	Some
Cotton wool	Very little
Bubble wrap	None

Which was the best sound muffler? ______________________

Name: ______________________ Date: __________

Class 4's report

Our challenge – How can you change the pitch of a string?

What we think – We think that the shorter the string, the higher the sound.

What we did –

- We made a model of a guitar neck.
- We put a paper cup at the end to help amplify the sound.
- We plucked the open string and used this sound as the starting point.
- We made the string shorter by about 2 cm each time and compared the sound.

Diagram –

Results – Every time we shortened the string, the sound changed.

Complete these sentences.

1 The longer the string, the ______________________.

2 The shorter the string, ______________________.

3 You play different notes on a guitar by

____

______________________.

Name: ______________________ Date: __________

Changing pitch

Kavya has a guitar.
It has strings. Some are thick strings and some are thin strings.
Kavya can tighten the strings or make them looser.
She uses her fingers to make the strings long or short.
She can pluck the strings hard or pluck them softly.
These all change the sound.

1 Use these words in the right places in the sentences below:

louder quieter higher lower

The shorter the string, the ______________ the sound.

The longer the string, the ______________ the sound.

The harder she plucks the string, the ______________ the sound.

The softer she plucks the string, the ______________the sound.

The tighter the string, the ______________ the sound.

The looser the string, the ______________ the sound.

The thicker the string, the ______________ the sound.

The thinner the string, the ______________ the sound.

2 Which of these words mean the same as vibrating?
Underline them.

flop judder quiver rock shake shudder tremble

Name: ______________________ Date: __________

Unit 7 assessment

1 Ali and Khaled use a tape recorder to play some music. Khaled played the music at different volumes. Ali recorded how far away she could hear the sounds. Here are their results.

Volume of tape recorder	1	2	3	4	5	6
Distance sound heard (m)	2	3	5		15	20

a) What material did the sound travel through to reach Aden's ears?

____

b) Fill in the missing result on the table.

2 Class 4 were investigating soundproofing. They measured how close to a box they needed to be to hear a clock ticking. Different materials were added to the box each time. Here are their results.

Materials	Empty box	Scrunched up paper	Bubble wrap	Carpet
Distance sound heard (m)	2.75	0.80	1.10	0.50

Which material was the best at soundproofing? ______________

3 Match each of these instruments to the way their sound is made.

Violin	Clarinet	Drum	Harp	Recorder

Vibrating string	Vibrating air in a tube	Vibrating skin

4 Riya has two elastic bands stretched over a tissue box. One is thicker than the other. Which band will give the lowest note? How can Riya make the thick elastic band make a higher note?

____

____